THE PRINCIPLE OF BALANCE

Story by: Adjwoa Tyehimba

Published by Melanin Origins

PO Box 122123; Arlington, TX 76012

All rights reserved, including the right of reproduction in whole

or in part in any form.

Copyright 2022

First Edition

The author asserts the moral right under the Copyright, Designs and Patents Act of 1988 to be identified as the author of this work.

This novel is a work of fiction. The names, characters and incidents portrayed in the work, other than those clearly in the public domain, are of the author's imagination and are not to be construed as real. Any resemblance to actual persons, living or dead, events or localities, is entirely coincidental.

All rights reserved. No part of this publication may be reproduced, stored in a retrieval system or transmitted, in any form by any means without the prior consent of the author, nor be otherwise circulated in any form of binding or cover other than that with which it is published and without a similar condition being imposed on the subsequent purchaser.

Series Editors: Reginald Robinson; Lenny Williams, & Shiree Fowler

Library of Congress Control Number: 2021942092

ISBN: 978-1-62676-519-1 hardback

ISBN: 978-1-62676-520-7 paperback

ISBN: 978-1-62676-521-4 ebook

THE PRINCIPLE OF BALANCE

"I will always strive to understand and respect the need to be complimentary; I will never be in conflict with myself or my family."

www.MelaninOrigins.com

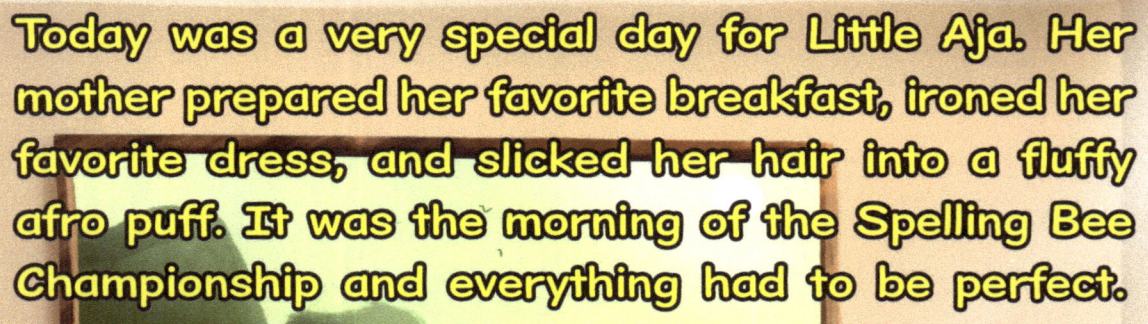

Today was a very special day for Little Aja. Her mother prepared her favorite breakfast, ironed her favorite dress, and slicked her hair into a fluffy afro puff. It was the morning of the Spelling Bee Championship and everything had to be perfect.

Aja made it to final round of the Spelling Bee at her school. She was confident, but the road was not easy. Aja stumbled on a few words during the last round, but this time she was ready.

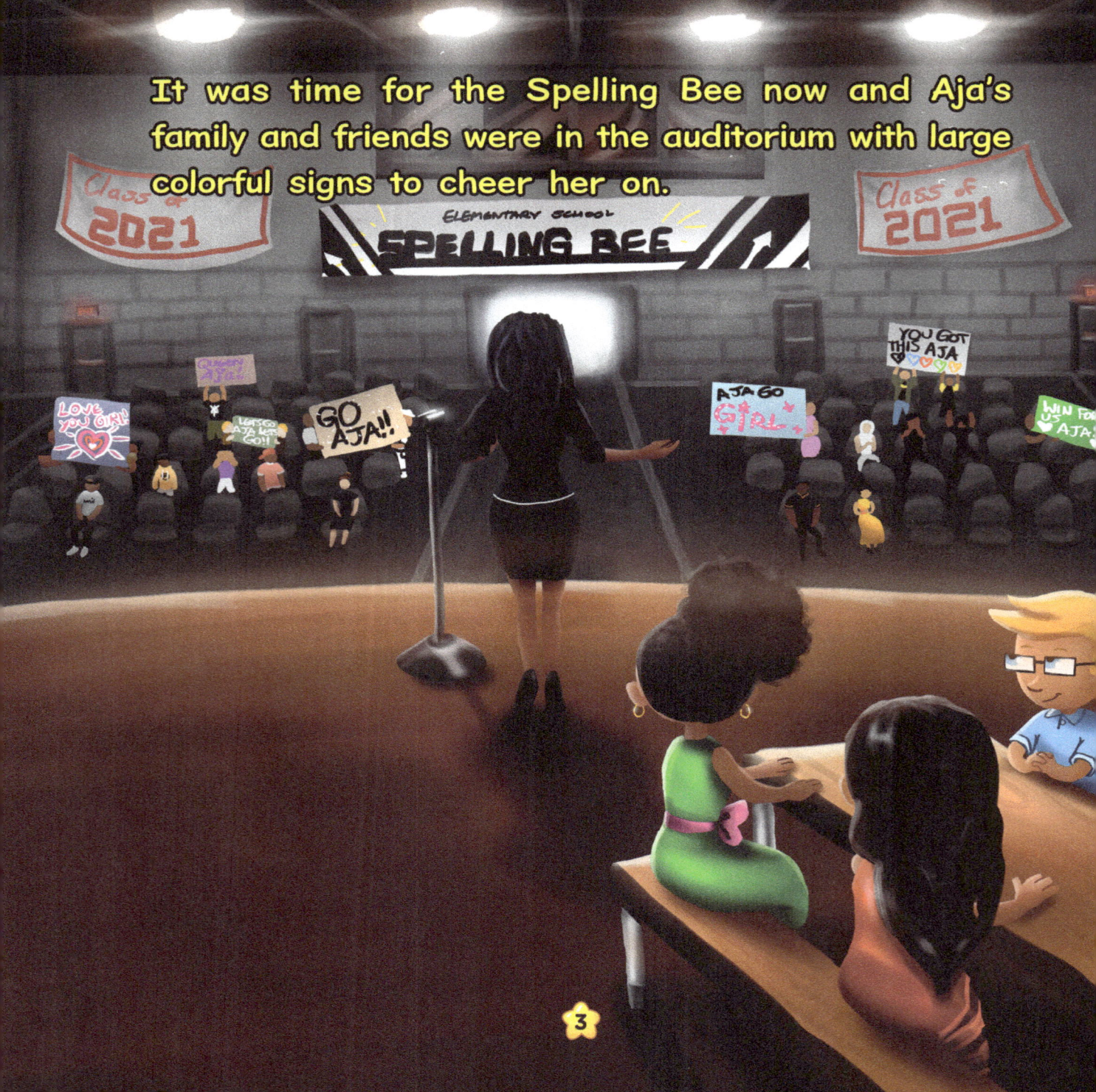
It was time for the Spelling Bee now and Aja's family and friends were in the auditorium with large colorful signs to cheer her on.

This was her turn to win it all. "Aja, spell Balance", said Principal MA'AT, who was serving as the judge. "Could you please use the word in a sentence?" asked Aja.

"B", Aja shouted as she recalled her father teaching her to ride a bike.

"A", she screamed as she thought about airplanes that use their wings to balance in the air.

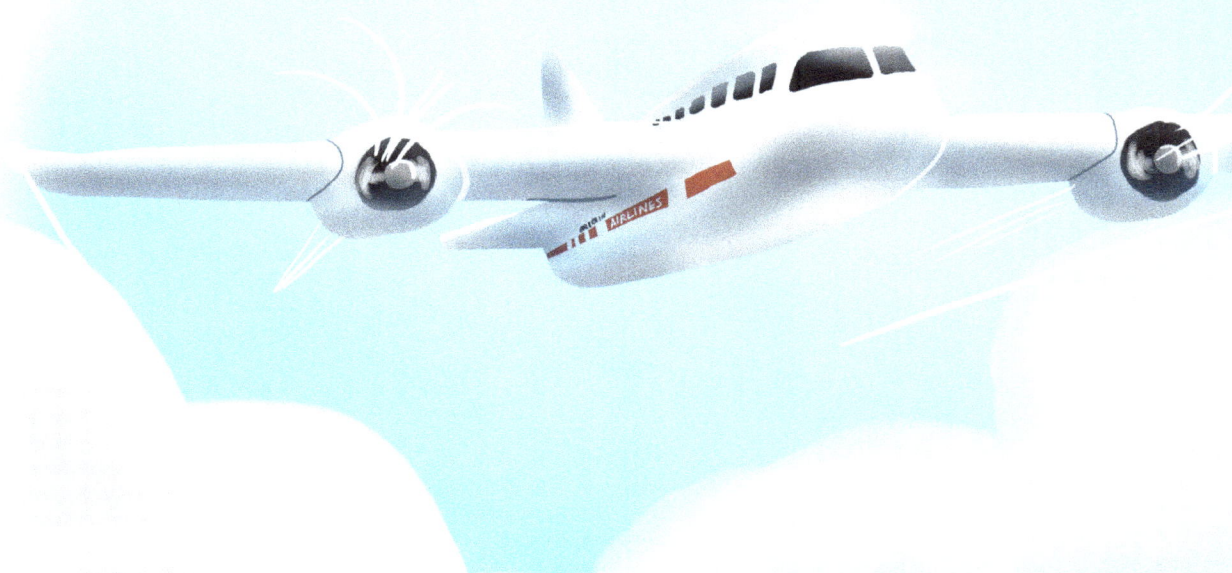

"L", she yelled as she remembered learning about the law of balance which meant for every negative there was a positive.

"A", she said. A letter which represented herself – Aja, and how she reminds herself to balance her video game time with a little study time.

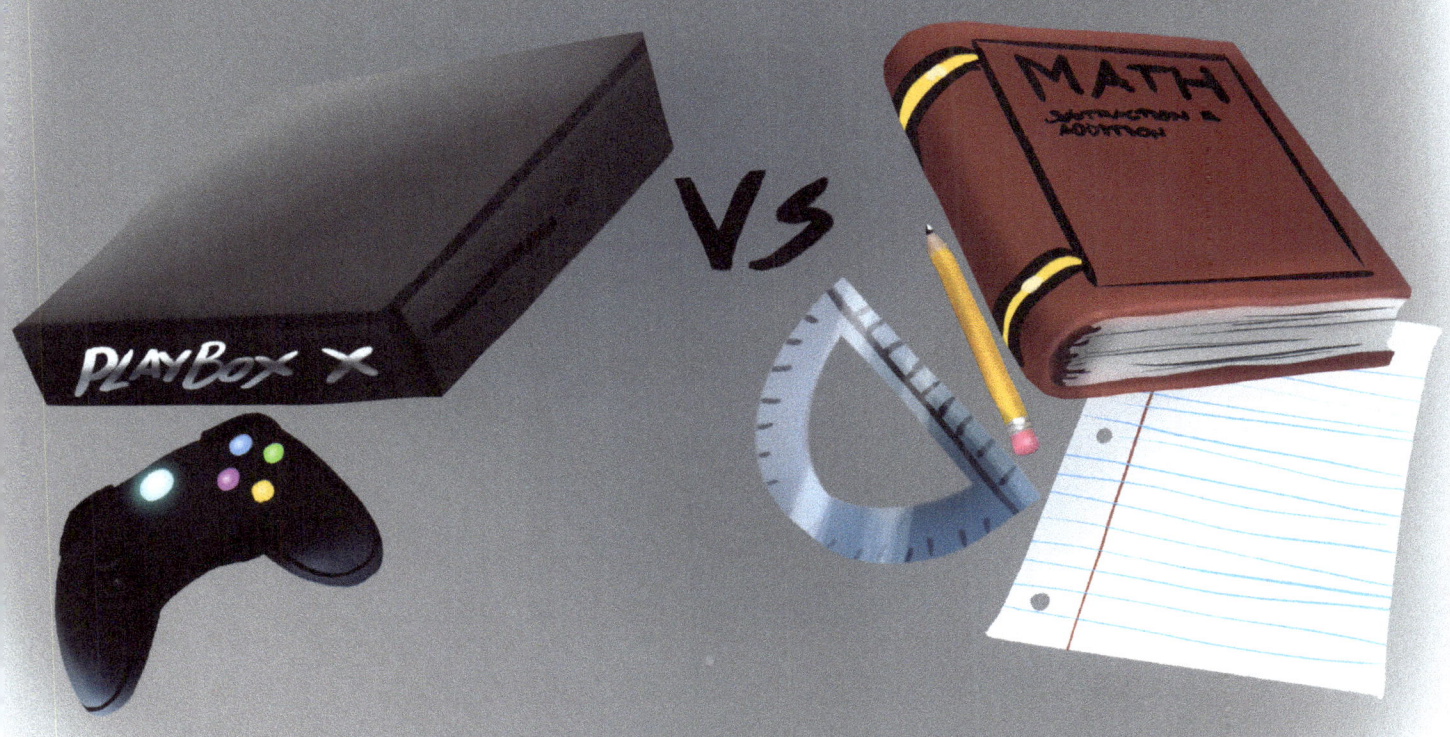

"N", is for nature. All animals, plants, and humans are important to one another and depend upon one another to achieve the circle of life and the balance of the world.

"C", stood for candy. Aja's mother does not allow her to eat candy before dinner, because children deserve to have a well-balanced meal before they eat anything sweet.

"E", she screamed as she realized she had math equations for homework that needed to be balanced out.

Aja opened her eyes, smiled, and shouted each letter once again with confidence, "B-A-L-A-N-C-E – Balance".

The crowd stood to their feet and began clapping in excitement! "Congratulations, Aja! You are the Spelling Bee Champion!" said Judge MA'AT as she handed Aja a beautiful trophy.

Aja had won her first spelling bee! She screamed in excitement, jumped for joy, and even did a cartwheel to celebrate!

Practicing balance gave Little Aja enough confidence to prepare for and win the Spelling Bee. Aja promised herself, from that day forward, that she would practice balance more often with family, friends, fun and, of course, studying.

Modern Day Melanin Origins

This book is dedicated to the Divine Mother of Holistic Health, Queen Afua.

Queen Afua is an **internationally renowned** best-selling author, holistic wellnessentrepreneur, and highly sought after natural health practitioner who guides men and women on a holistic transformational journey of wellness.

With over 40 years of experience, Queen Afua has built a **Wellness Empire** that includes: The Queen Afua Wellness Center and bestselling books *Sacred Woman: A Guide to Healing the Feminine Body, Mind, and Spirit* as well as *Man Heal Thyself.*

~ QueenAfua.com

www.ingramcontent.com/pod-product-compliance
Lightning Source LLC
Chambersburg PA
CBHW040014080526
44586CB00028B/2999